My Village,
STURBRIDGE

My Village, STURBRIDGE

GARY BOWEN

Wood engravings designed by Gary Bowen
and engraved by Randy Miller

FARRAR, STRAUS AND GIROUX

❀ *New York* ❀

For Ruthina

G.B.

My Village,
STURBRIDGE

August 23, 1827

Isaiah Thomas, Esq.
Printing Office
Worcester, Massachusetts

Most honorable Mr. Thomas:

I have completed this series of wood engravings
of views of my village, Sturbridge, as an appren-
tice in your printing office here. Mr. Ewing, the
master engraver, has advised me to show this work
to you.

Mr. Wight, our gristmiller, told me if the water wheel rotates ten times each minute, the millstone will revolve one hundred times. I am amazed that a 3,000-pound granite stone can have such marvelous governed haste. He expects that the hard edge of his newly imported French buhrstone will provide greater efficiency in grinding our community's corn, wheat, and rye.

This is my brother, George, who is putting snow on the bridge so it can be crossed by sleigh. He is younger than I.

I have never entered this tavern. Mother has explained to us that strong drink is a foe to peace and love. It makes a man idle, wicked, and poor and ofttimes drives him crazy. My teacher avows: "Obey this lesson. Touch not! Taste not! Rum, gin, brandy, and whiskey lead to poverty, idleness, vice, and disgrace."

Will Towne and I often spied the British from the monitor windows that skirt his attic. The "British," in truth, were sheep on the common. I sighted the parson's home from the same windows, for my engraving of his house.

16.

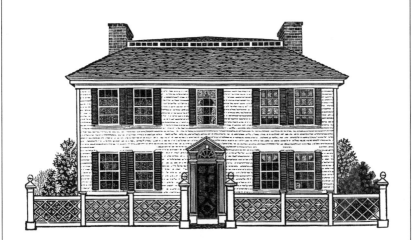

I have played the Townes' pianoforte; they have a pipe organ, to boot. It is in this very house that the Masons have meetings. My father attended, my grandfather always.

Asa Knight's new store has proven to be a supplier of the unusual. Silks, ivory combs, coinsilver spoons, and even my writing quills are all there for trade. We have found his Shaker seeds to be of exceptional quality.

Our teacher has never lived with us. However, as payment for George's and my schooling, we provide two cords of wood. Winter illnesses have kept the school attendance very low for the past two years. Fortunately, I have had good health.

The Fennos' home was the first two-over-two house built in our village, back in 1704. They still use quantities of woodenware and a Betty lamp, which yields poor light and a frightful odor, since they burn only cooking grease.

John McClellan has in his law office the most
extraordinary number of books I have ever seen.
Some of them contain engraved illustrations, which
have been a source of inspiration.

Three generations of the Fitch family remodeled and made additions to this house. They have a granite fireplace, uncommon to my village, as well as a beautifully stenciled floor.

I remember my grandfather looking very much like this when he cast pewter. He developed an exceptional formula, composed of tin, antimony, and copper, which when heated to the proper temperature produced a pewter of extreme hardness, a quality everyone thought to be most desirable.

Mother estimates that it would take 160 hours for her to card twenty pounds of wool, which the carding mill could more thoroughly blend in one hour's time. Since we have been bringing our wool to the mill, we have leisure time in the evenings. Mine is devoted to drawing and engraving.

Silas Freeman's house is the only house in the village that has running water inside. The water is gravity-fed from the spring through sumac stocks to the sink in their buttery. Mother says that indoor running water would be a miraculous aid to housekeeping. Silas's father was a ship's cooper and has a small cooper shop on their farm.

Our maple trees provide enough sap to satisfy our sugar needs, but now and then we trade for white sugar cones at Mr. Knight's store. Mother prefers white sugar to maple when baking special cakes.

Mr. Lees, the tinsmith, who is a Mason, imports all of his sheet tin from England. The most distinctive item he makes is a double sunburst lantern of his own design. Mrs. Lees decorates some of his document boxes, teapots, and other containers with oil paints.

Our blacksmith constructed this stone building himself. The bellows came from the city, but the rest of the tools he forged. Most blacksmiths find locks and keys too difficult a task, but they are his specialty.

The broommakers hire boys after school to pound pegs and cut broomcorn. My brother worked two weeks for them; his pay, a broom. Having collected the seeds from that broom, we hope to grow enough corn next year to make our own.

Our new parson believes that a red parsonage is a hindrance to spiritual thought and he is positive that this is why the last minister was compelled to leave Sturbridge. He has preached that the community's spirit would be purified if our parsonage were painted white.

The school children's ditty:

> *The parson's house*
> *Is red, not white.*
> *Dread color keeps*
> *Him up all night.*

Hervey Brooks fired his kiln eleven times his first year here, burning a total of 110 cords. Last October I cut a cord and helped with the firing, in trade for milk pans for Mother. He told me he made one hundred twelve of those redware pans in a day. Mr. Brooks explained he has time only to make utilitarian pieces, but with great care.

Once, Quaker friends invited me to an assembly at their meetinghouse. I found it surprising that the Quakers have no minister to give a sermon. The elders presided over the meeting, but anyone could "speak as the spirit moves."

Father always bid for a family pew in our church. Since his passing, we have not been able to afford such fine seats, but we use the free seats in the gallery. Sometimes I pump the organ.

I am presenting my work to you, Mr. Thomas, with the hope that you will allow me to continue my apprenticeship at your Sturbridge printing office. I have been apprenticed there for three years.

I feel strongly that illustrated publications will be of great importance in the future. And so it is with all earnestness that I desire to become a master engraver.

Yours sincerely,

True Mason

Sturbridge,

Massachusetts

Old Sturbridge Village, the living museum in Sturbridge, Massachusetts, is representative of a typical New England farm community of the early nineteenth century. O.S.V. appears to be an authentic village that has been preserved intact, but actually it is a collection of buildings and artifacts from all over New England, accumulated by two brothers, Albert B. and J. Cheney Wells, of Southbridge, Massachusetts. The buildings were brought together at their present site in 1936 through the efforts of Albert's son, George B. Wells.

An inspiring educational tool, Old Sturbridge Village dramatically displays the simple life of our skillful and self-reliant ancestors. Visitors stand fascinated as they watch the Village "interpreters," dressed in period clothes, demonstrating the arts and crafts characteristic of the time.

True Mason, the hero of this book, is a fictional character, but Isaiah Thomas (1749–1831) is a real figure in American history. He was apprenticed to a printer at the age of six, was managing the shop at twelve, and at twenty-one founded a newspaper, the *Massachusetts Spy*. He became the leading American publisher after the Revolution and was noted for his children's books, textbooks, almanacs, dictionaries, and Bibles. His various related enterprises in Worcester, Massachusetts, employed one hundred and fifty people, who operated seven printing presses and a bindery, as well as a bookstore. Many of Mr. Thomas's apprentices became his partners and established newspapers and bookstores from Maine to Georgia and as far west as the Mississippi. His Worcester printing office, built in 1783, is now part of Old Sturbridge Village.